My First Holy Qur'an
Coloring Book and Reader

Condensed and Simplified by
Yahiya Emerick

With illustrations by Patricia Meehan

© Copyright 2013 Yahiya Emerick

All Rights reserved. No part of this book may be reproduced or transmitted in any form, or by any means, electronic or mechanical, including photocopying and recording, or by any information storage retrieval system, without permission in writing from the publisher.

ISBN: 1494345560
EAN-13: 978-1494345563

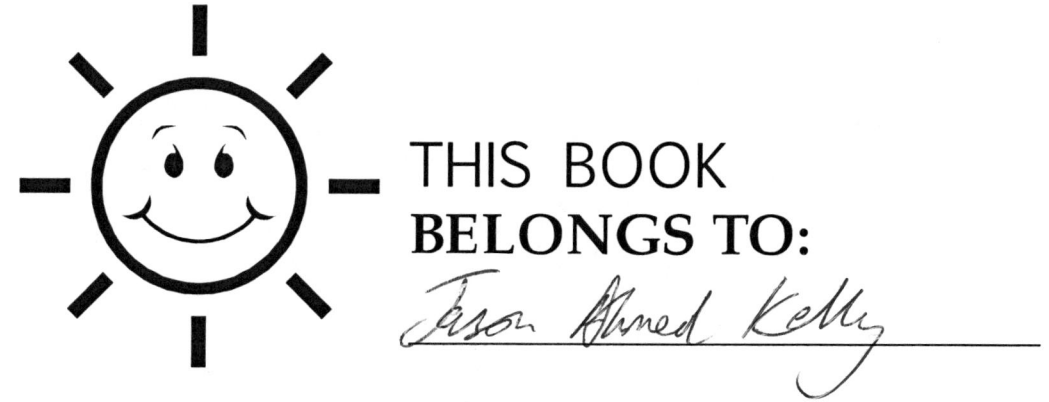

THIS BOOK BELONGS TO:
Jason Ahmed Kelly

Bismillahir Rahmanir Rahim

In the Name of Allah,
The Caring and the Merciful.

My First Holy Qur'an

Coloring Book and Reader

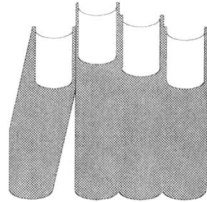 **Reading for Comprehension.**
Textbooks for Today and Tomorrow.
The Islamic Arts Series

Grade Range 2-4

By Yahiya Emerick

Illustrated by Patricia Meehan

Reading for Comprehension: Textbooks for Today and Tomorrow, is a new effort to present information on Muslims and Islam in a manner which is in keeping with current educational standards.

This coloring book for young children is meant to be a supplementary teaching tool for use in a lower elementary classroom. It uses the seven categories of the *Emaan ul Mufassil* to explore topics mentioned in the Holy Qur'an. Simple rhymes coupled with simplified text from the translation of the Qur'an in English bring the basics of the Qur'anic message alive for the very young. Coloring activities reinforce the texts. Parents and teachers are encouraged to use this book as enrichment to teach lessons on the Qur'an, Islam and life in general. See our website at www.ifna.net for more educational resources.

Dear Children,

 Our religion is Islam. We are Muslims. Our book is the Holy Qur'an and our Messenger is Muhammad, peace be upon him.

We learn about our religion from the Qur'an and also from the life and sayings of the Messenger.

There are seven main areas of Islamic teachings. The seven things are mentioned in a sentence called the *Emaan ul-Mufassil* (the beliefs in detail).

Here it is written below, first in Arabic sounds, and then the meaning in English:

"Amantu bil lahi, wa mala-ikatihi wa kutoobihi was rasoolihi wal yowm ul akhiri wal qadri, khayrihi wa sharihi min Allahi ta'ala wal ba'ithi ba'ad al mowt."

"I believe in **Allah**, His **Angels**, His **Books**, His **Messengers**, the **Last Day**, and in **Measurement** (of the things in life) and that both the good and the bad (of it) come from Allah and in **Life after Death**."

This book that you hold in your hands will take these seven beliefs and explore them using the Qur'an as our guide.

As you read the concepts and verses from the Qur'an, think about how you can make them a part of your life.

You can also have fun coloring the pictures too! May Allah help us and guide us to be the best Muslims ever! *Ameen!*

In the Name of Allah,
the Caring, and the Merciful

Who is Allah?

Allah is the Creator

Allah brings us the light

Allah loves all the people

Allah loves what is right

This is how you write the name of Allah in Arabic. Can you color it in?

We cannot see Allah

His power is too great

We can see what he does

In all the day and night

Allah made everything that you can see

The birds, the stars, the water, the trees

He made our world nice for us to live

Allah is never afraid to give

Allah has special powers

That only He knows how to use

He told us in his holy book

Just what he has to do

We work so hard then go to sleep

Because we need to rest

Allah is strong and never sleeps

Because He is the best

From Surah 2, Ayah 255
What is Allah Like?

In the Name of Allah,
the Caring, and the Merciful

Allah! There is no other god except for Him.
   (He is) the Living, and the Forever!
   He never gets tired, and (He does need to) rest.

Everything in the heavens and the earth belongs to Him;
   who can do or say anything without His permission?

   He knows what is in front of (people in the future)
      and what they have left behind (in their past),
      while they have none of what He knows
      except for what He lets them.

(The power of) His throne goes over the heavens
   and the earth, and He never gets tired
   in keeping them safe.

He alone is the Most High,
   the One Who is Most Great. [255]

1. What are two words used to describe Allah?

2. What are two things that Allah knows about people?

3. Why do you think Allah never needs to rest or sleep?

Allah gave us a prayer

We say it everyday

He told us how to ask Him

For His help in every way

Surah 1
The Special Prayer

In the Name of Allah,
the Caring, and the Merciful [1]

All the best words are for Allah,
   the Lord of All the Worlds;
   (He is) the Caring, and the Merciful
   and the Master of the Day of Judgment. [2-4]

You are the only One we work for,
   and You are the only One we ask for help. [5]

Show us the best way to live (so we can be good):
   the same way as those you are already happy with,
   not (the way) of those You are angry with,
   and not (the way) of those who went astray. [6-7]

---

1. What are two words that were used to describe Allah?

2. Why do we want to know the best way to live?

Muslims Pray to Allah

Allah wants people to be safe

Allah knows the dangers we face

Allah sees us all the time

So be good in every place

Muslims help people who need it

Allah needs no helpers

No friends or partners to win

He is the one and only

And we only pray to Him

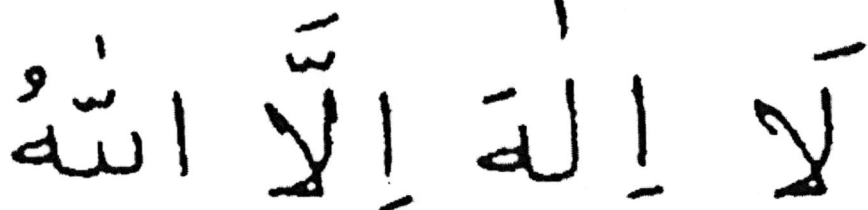

We say:
There is no god but Allah!

La ila ha ill Allah

Surah 112
Allah is Only One

In the Name of Allah,
the Caring, and the Merciful

Say (to the people) that Allah is One God -
Allah is the Forever Everything.

He never gives birth and He was never born,
And there is nothing the same as Him! [1-4]

A Muslim believes in Allah!
All Muslims are Brothers and Sisters

Tell people that Allah is one!

---

1. How many gods are there?

2. Is there anything the same as Allah?

3. What should you say to someone who says that there are many gods?

Word Search

Vocabulary about Allah

```
L L Y L W C K U C H H S S E N
P O U U H U E G T J Q K Q N V
L Y V F N A A M E R I A F O L
F L H I R G N I V I G R O F D
R O P C N E A W N M V C V E J
E R R R R G W H C I M C E E U
T D B E R Y N O A S M H X E S
S C Y M V Y F O P L W A N U T
A R O T A E R C R A L O Z N I
M G I V E R R J T T R A T S C
Y K N O W I N G E H S A T E E
A L I V I N G D T K Q A U E C
O H O L M A P L I W E L O N A
V O A H G Y N N A R J V G T E
O B U D D V D D G A E P O X P
```

Names to Find and Circle

The words can be in any direction!

Hint: look for the first two letters of a word together!

AHAD, ALLAH, CREATOR, EMAAN, EXALTED, FAIR, FOREVER, FORGIVING, GIVER, GREAT, HOLY, JUSTICE, KIND, KNOWING, LIVING, LORD, LOVING, MASTER, MERCIFUL, ONE, PEACE, POWERFUL, STRONG, TAQWA, TAWHEED, THRONE, UNSEEN

Who are the Angels?

Allah made many creatures

The birds, the fish and snails

He also made nice turtles

And sheep and dogs and quails

Allah made all the people

In every land and place

He wants us to be friends

And live our lives in peace

Surah 49, Ayah 13
People Must Live In Peace

In the Name of Allah,
the Caring, and the Merciful

All you people! We created you from a single
   (pair of) a male and a female and made you
   into different races and tribes so you can
   come to know one another.

The best among you in the sight of Allah
   is the one who is the most sincere
   (about his or her duty to obey Him). For sure,
   Allah knows all and is aware. [13]

___

1. Why did Allah make us all different?

2. Who is the best person?

We must respect each other!
Allah loves all people!

Some people just don't listen

They want to be mean and bad

Allah gets very angry

When he sees the people sad

SUICIDE BOMBER...

Some people do bad things and cause trouble.

Allah hates for people to do bad things to others!

Allah created Jinns

Another kind of thing

They are almost like people

But they're made of smokeless flames

Jinns are invisible and are made of fire energy

We cannot see the jinns

But they can see us

Some of them are really bad

And they whisper to mess us up

Jinns tell people to be bad
and to do bad things!
Some people forget Allah
and listen to the jinns!

The biggest jinn is really bad

A mean and nasty one!

He's called Shaytan and only wants

To keep us far from home

Allah had said, "Don't eat the apple"

And the first man and his wife did

This was the first trick of Shaytan

And many more are hid

Shaytan is mad because Allah said that People were better than Jinns!

Surah 17, Ayat 61-65
How does Shaytan Attack Us?

In the Name of Allah,
the Caring, and the Merciful

When We told the angels, "*Bow down (in respect) to Adam,*" they all bowed down. But Iblis, (who was a jinn that was there watching, did not bow down along with them).

"*How can I bow down to a thing that You made from mud?*" he asked. [61]

"*Look at that!*" he continued. "*This (human) is the one who You're honoring over me! If You give me a chance until the Day of Assembly, I'll make his children blindly obedient (to me), all but a few!*" [62]

"*Go away,*" (Allah) said to him, "*and if any of them follow you, then Hellfire will be enough of a reward for you all!* [63]

"Trick any of them that you can with your (charming) voice (of temptation). Attack them with your cavalry and with your soldiers.

"Share in their wealth and children (by making them think it's okay to lie and steal for money and family), and make promises to them - even though the promises of Shaytan are nothing more than lies. [64]

"As for My servants, however, you will have no power over them. Your Lord is (powerful) enough to take care (of them)." [65]

Shaytan uses bad things to trick people into forgetting about Allah!

Fight the Shaytan by asking Allah to help you against him!

Allah created other things

Besides animals, plants and jinns

He made a group of servants

And these angels help us win

Angels watch us and write down what we do!

The Angels watch over us

To see our good and bad

They always report to Allah

And don't feel lonely or sad

The angels write about us in their books!
They write our good and bad deeds.
They are made of energy from light!

The Angels are always good

And they do what Allah says

Sometimes they bring us messages

Or comfort us when we're sad

They record all our good and bad deeds

In a special book they have

They'll bring this book right back to us

On a Day when we'll be either happy or sad

Angels can go anywhere in the world and up in space. The can go all over the place!

Surah 3, Ayat 42-48
How did the Angels Complete a Mission?

In the Name of Allah,
the Caring, and the Merciful

The angels (appeared) to Maryam and said, *"Maryam! Allah has chosen you and purified you. He has chosen you above the women of all nations, so be obedient to your Lord, prostrate yourself, and bow down with those who bow (before Allah)."* [42-43]

(This story) that We're revealing to you, (Muhammad), was unknown (to you before), for you weren't there when the (male relatives) chose reeds randomly to decide who among them must provide (money to support) Maryam, and you certainly weren't there when they argued (over the results). [44]

When the angels (again returned to Maryam after some time had passed), they said, "Maryam! Allah gives you the good news of a word from Him. He's going to be called the Messiah, 'Esa (Jesus), the son of Maryam. He will be honored in this world, as well as in the next, where he will be among those nearest (to Allah)." [45]

"He will speak to people in childhood and also when he's grown, and he's going to be one of the morally righteous." [46]

"But my Lord!" she cried out. "How can I have a son when no man has come near me?"

"And so it is that Allah creates whatever He wants," the angels replied. "When He decides something, He only has to say, 'Be' and it is." [47]

"He will teach him the holy writings and fill him with wisdom (by teaching him) the Torah and the Gospel. [48]

---

1. What nice thing did the angel say to Maryam when he first came?

2. What gift from Allah was she going to have?

We cannot see the angels

But they are always there

They're with us when we're sleeping

And they're with us at our prayers

The angels also go to the Masjid for Salah!

The angels can go up to the sky and heaven!
They fight the bad jinns and keep them out!

The Story of the Boy Who Stopped the Shaytan

Ali saw an old woman.
She had a big basket.
She needed help.

The old lady was happy.

The basket was heavy.
Ali was getting tired.

A Shaytan came close.
The Shaytans are bad.
They want us to be bad.

The Shaytan told Ali to run away.
He said go and do fun things.
Do not help the old lady.

Ali remembered how to make the Shaytan go away.
Do you know what he said?
"Allah protect me from the bad Shaytan!"
"Owzubil lah himina shaytan ir rajeem!"

The old lady said to put the basket in the house.
She was very happy with Ali.
Ali did a good deed.

The old lady gave some food to Ali.
Ali was very happy.

Ali said thank you to Allah.
Allah was very happy with Ali.
Ali stopped the Shaytan with Allah's help.

Word Search
Famous Angels and their Jobs

```
J F A X P F N D J D A O
L I X V A W O V R Y R A
U U B I N V I S I B L E
L I A R Z A T N Q V P B
G Y L I A G A U G B S L
R G I S I E L N E S E M
S R G R W J E Q O G I Z
O E H A Z F V L N K A L
G N T F M E E A A N W N
Y E Y I U M R I W W A Y
H D S L R O L D E E D S
M V F V W W J R J S V O
```

Names to Find and Circle

The words can be in any direction!

Hint: look for the first two letters of a word together!

ANGEL, AZRAIL, DEEDS, ENERGY, INVISIBLE, ISRAFIL
JIBRAEEL, LIGHT, MIKAIL,
REVELATION, WINGS, WRITES

What are the Books of Allah?

Allah does not talk to people openly

His angels bring His messages honestly

Sometimes the messages say

"Here take a quick look!"

Other times they fill up a whole book!

The Angel who brings
the messages is named "Jibraeel"

Surah 42, Ayat 51-53
What Does Allah Say about the Qur'an?

In the Name of Allah,
the Caring, and the Merciful

Allah will not speak to a living person directly, unless it's through inspired revelation, (inspiration) from behind a veil, or through the action of a message-bringer (like an angel), who will reveal, by Allah's permission, whatever Allah wants him to, for He is High and wise. [51]

And so it is that We're inspiring you, (Muhammad,) through (the work of Jibraeel,) a spirit (under) Our command. You didn't know what revelation and faith were before.

We've sent down to you a light, which you can use to guide whomever of Our servants that We will.

You're offering guidance (to people) that will take (them) towards a straight path - *(towards) the path of Allah.*

(He is) the One Who owns everything in the heavens and everything on the earth, and all matters (of good and bad) will go back to Allah (for deciding). [52-53]

Only special people called Messengers get whole books. Do you remember the name of the angel who brings the messages?

Allah gave many books to people

Back in the olden days

After a while some got lost

But some books stayed

Allah loves for people to read and learn

Shaytan was always up to his old tricks

He wanted to make people forget Allah

And to worship false gods

Made of stones and sticks

A lot of people think they can make their own gods from sticks and stones. This is wrong!

Allah sent His books

To tell people the truth

He wants everyone to know

How to be good

And follow the straight path

There are two roads in life:
The high road leads to Allah,
and the low road leads to a bad place
where bad people are punished

The Qur'an is the last book Allah sent

In it He said everything He meant

The older books were lost or changed

The Qur'an is the last one Allah arranged

The Qur'an tells us about Allah.
It tells stories of special people.

Read the Qur'an every day
So you know how to live the best way!

Surah 10, Ayat 1-10
How does Shaytan Attack Us?

In the Name of Allah,
the Caring, and the Merciful

Alif. Lām. Rā.

These are the verses of the Book of Wisdom. [1]

Is it so strange to people that We've sent Our inspiration to a man from among themselves, so he could warn people (of Allah's judgment) and give the good news to the believers that they can have their place in the sight of their Lord? Yet, the people who don't believe say (of it), *"This (Qur'an) is clearly all just magic!"* [2]

Your Lord is Allah, the One Who created the heavens and the earth in six stages. Then He set Himself upon the throne (of power) and began making commands. There are none who can speak up (for you) other than those He allows. That's your Lord Allah, so serve Him.

Won't you take a reminder? [3]

All of you will return back to Him, and Allah's promise is true. He's the One Who began the process of creation and then keeps doing it, so that He can fairly reward those who believe and do what's right.

Those who reject Him will be made to drink boiling mud, and they'll have a painful punishment because of their rejection (of the truth). [4]

He's the One Who caused the sun to glow brightly with multiple (colors) and (He caused) the moon to be lit up (at night). He measured out (the moon's) stations, so you could keep track of the years and the passage (of time).

Allah didn't create (all of these things) except for a true purpose, and He explains His verses to people who understand. [5]

Truly, in the changing of night and day and in everything that Allah created in the heavens and the earth, are proofs for those who are mindful (of Him). [6]

Those who don't look forward to their meeting with Us, who are satisfied with the life of this world and who ignore Our (revealed) verses - they're going to have their home in the Fire on account of what they've earned for themselves. [7-8]

On the other hand, those who believe and do what's right will be guided by their Lord because of their faith – rivers will flow beneath them in gardens of delight! [9]

Their prayer in (the garden) will be,
"*Glory be to You,   O Allah!*"

Their greetings will be, "*Peace,*" and they'll end their prayers by saying, "*Praise be to Allah, the Lord of All the Worlds!*" [10]

Those who read and follow the Qur'an are rewarded with a beautiful place in the next life.

This is Rasheed.

He reads the Qur'an every day.

He is learning how to read it in Arabic.

He also reads the meanings in English.

Who are the Messengers?

Allah sent books to special people

Who are called Messengers

After sharing what they found

Their followers spread

Their message all around!

People share the words of Allah

Sometimes the people

Didn't want to hear

And they bothered the Messengers

And their friends and left them in fear

Allah rewards the Messengers

And believers who had to fight

Some of them struggled

And fought with all their might!

Surah 2, Ayah 213
How did the First Books Get Lost?

In the Name of Allah,
the Caring, and the Merciful

All people were once a single community, and Allah raised messengers among them to give glad tidings (of Paradise) and also warnings (of Hellfire). However, He also sent the books of truth to be a judge between people in their disputes.

However, after the clear proof came to them, those who received these (earlier) revealed books, out of division and pride, fell into disagreement.

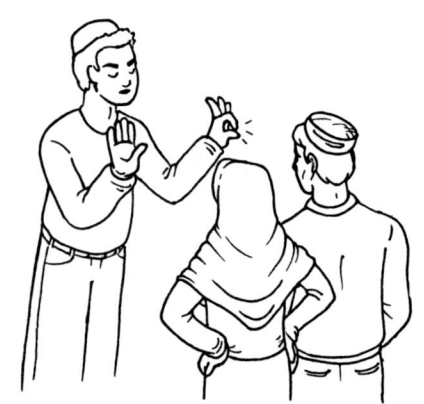

Yet, because of His kindness, Allah guided the sincere believers out of their disputes and brought them to the truth, for Allah guides whomever He wants towards a straight path. [213]

Word Search

Famous Prophets and Messengers

```
A Y Y O U B S C M N E P D N I
S H D J S A X E Z A B S F U D
Y H D A L I E A S M C M A H K
U P U E M H R U Y Y S U N U Y
S N H A A M M D Z A Y I H A Y
U X K R Y N A A I L Q D C M O
F T B X X B L H K U N U V A P
H I H S N Y H M U S B W B D I
T U N U A E Z D H M P A Y A S
D Y R S Z Y L U T F Y D P O M
G A A Z F P L N E V E T X S A
H M C F B A Y I M X W X O C I
F B T Z J K I S H A Q L U Q L
W R Q T Z F P K L Q F E L W A
M O V N Y H A Y Y I R A K A Z
```

Names to Find and Circle

The words can be in any direction!

Hint: look for the first two letters of a word together!

ADAM, ALYASA, AYYOUB, DAWUD, ESA, HARUN, HUD, IBRAHEEM, IDRIS, ILYAS, ISHAQ, ISMAIL, LUT, MUHAMMAD, MUSA, NUH, SALEH, SHUAYB, SULAYMAN, YAHIYA, YAQUB, YUNUS, YUSUF, ZAKARIYYAH

There were five Messengers

Whom we know the best

They got the biggest books

Bigger than all the rest!

They were:

Ibraheem, Musa, Dawud

'Esa and Muhammad

Peace be upon them all!

We listen to the stories of the Messengers and Prophets and learn from their adventures

Ibraheem lived a long time ago

His father made idols for sale

And this made Ibraheem sad

He wanted to find the true God

So he went to a faraway land

Ibraheem told his family to pack their bags and go with him on a long journey to obey Allah

Allah showed Ibraheem the way

He even asked Ibraheem to give

The life of his son away!

But Allah stopped Ibraheem

Before it was too late

He wanted to show him

How to be true and straight

Prophet Musa had a really hard life

His enemies took him as a baby

And made him a prince

Allah showed him the way out to be safe

And the army of Egypt

Was wiped out all over the place

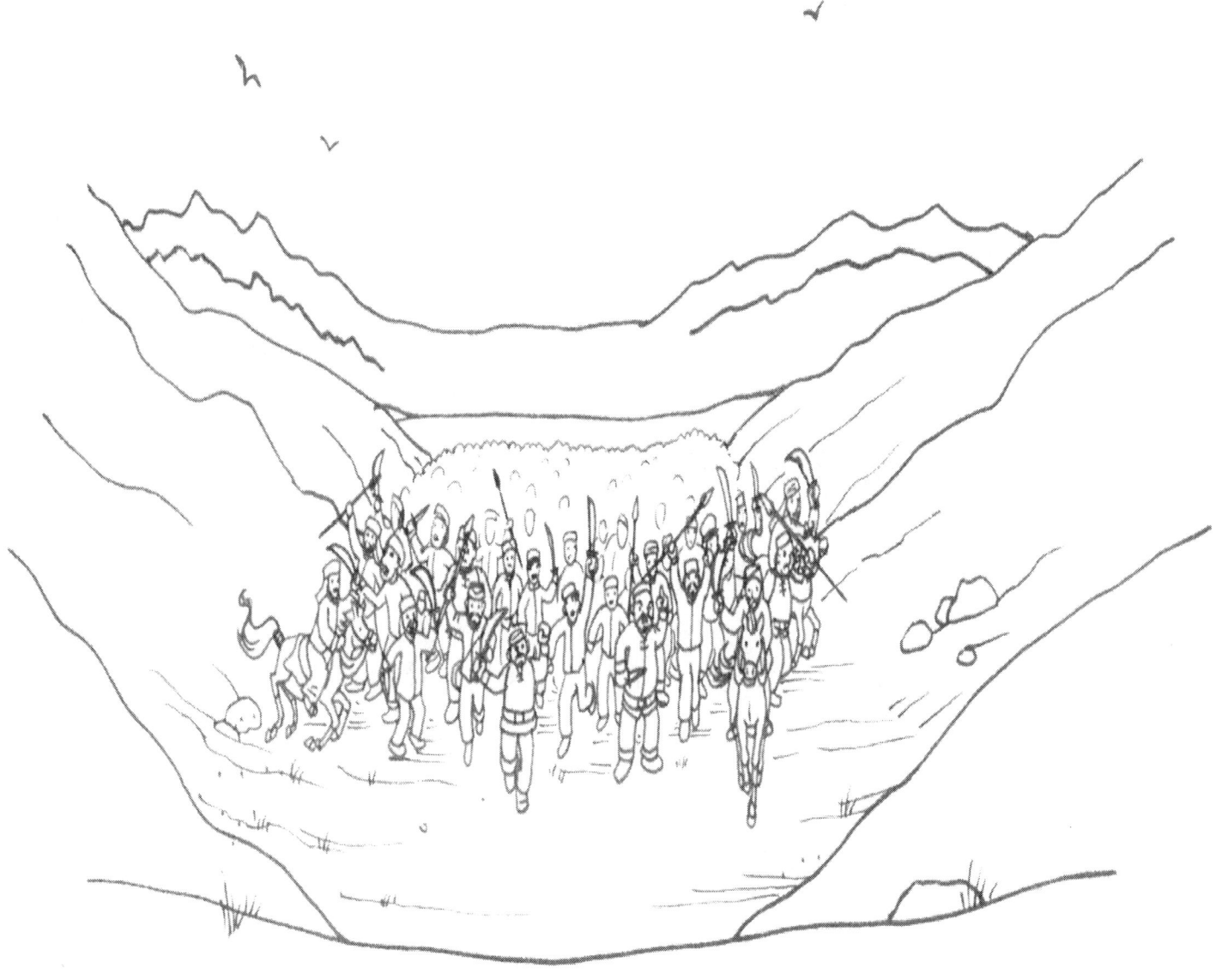

Allah made the waves crash on to the army of the king of Egypt

Prophet Musa saved a lot of people

They followed him to be free

But they never really listened

They argued over every little thing

Allah called Musa away

To give him a special book

But his people were fooled by Shaytan

Who said, "Make an idol."

That was all it took!

The people made a statue of a cow from melted gold jewelry. Allah was angry with them!

After that Allah was angry

He gave them a lot of laws

They had to learn to listen

And not be full of flaws

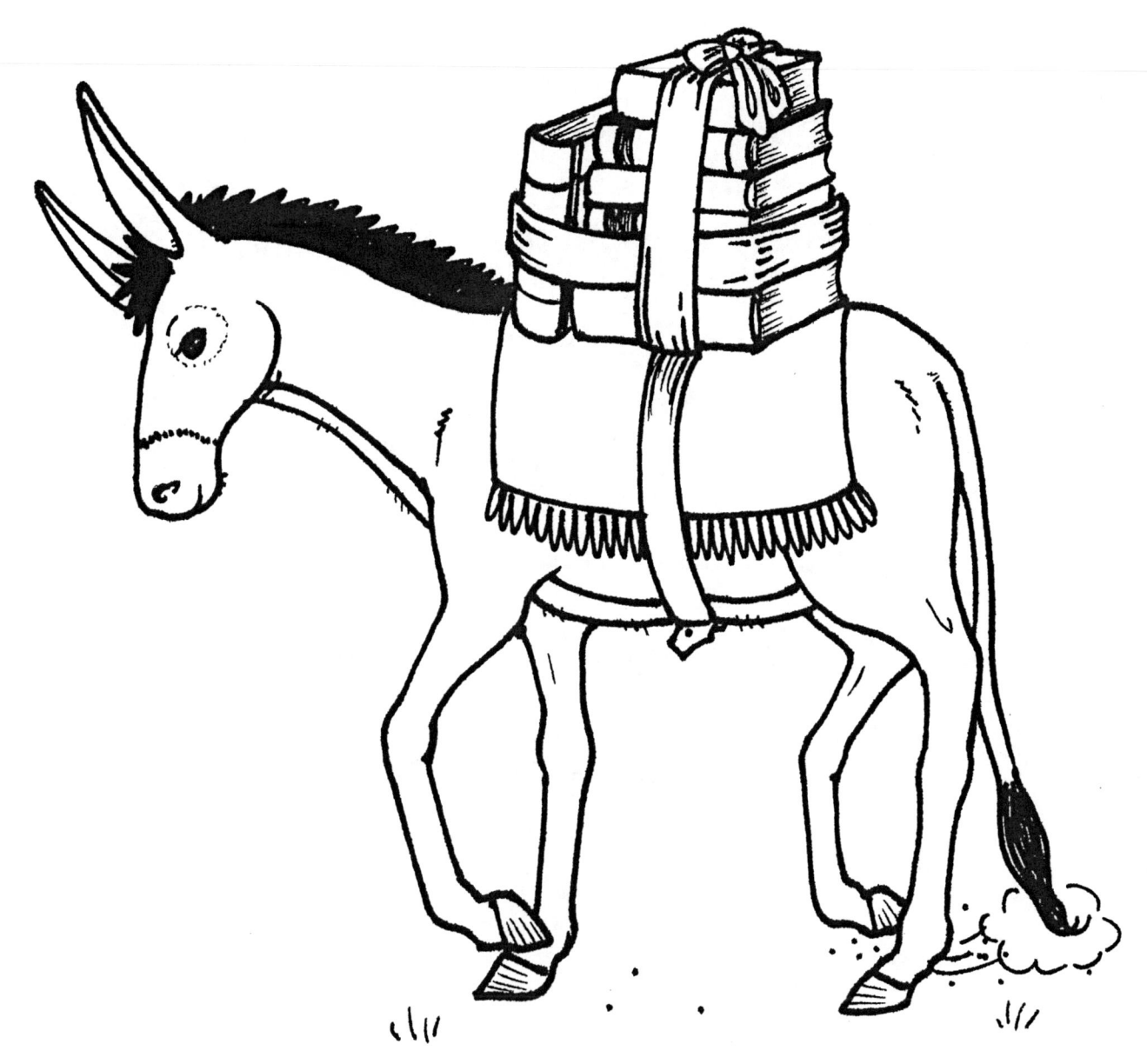

The people of Musa were given so many laws
That they fill up many books!

Dawud was a young shepherd boy

He was brave when

his people were scared

He faced a giant named Jalut

And knocked him down

With rocks shot in the air

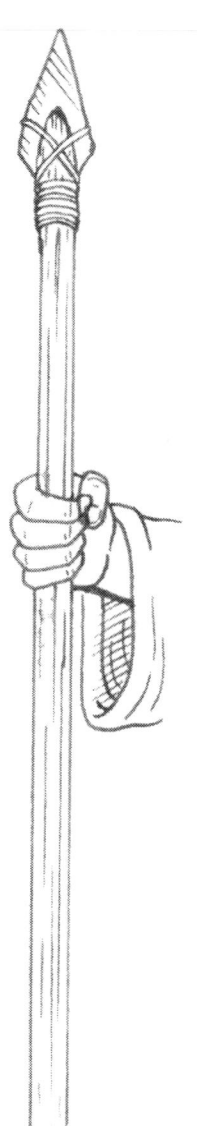
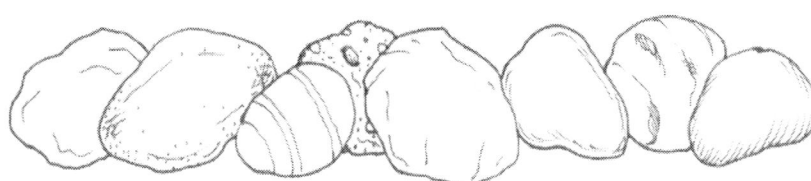

Dawud used small stones in his slingshot to knock out the giant warrior named Jalut!

His people made him their king!

Dawud was made a very wise king

He wrote music, poetry and other things

He solved many problems he saw

And he never forgot that

Allah gave him it all!

Dawud was the king of the city of Jerusalem

Surah 38, Ayat 17-26
How did Allah Teach Dawud to be Patient?

In the Name of Allah,
the Caring, and the Merciful

Have patience with what they're saying. Remember (the example of) Our servant Dawud, the sturdy one, for he always turned (to Allah). [17]

We tamed the hills and made them declare Our glory along with him throughout the evening and at the rising of the day. [18]

The gathered birds turned along with him (to praise Allah), as well. We strengthened his rule and granted him wisdom and good sense in his talks. [19-20]

Have you ever heard the story of the arguers? They climbed over the wall of his private chamber and came to him.

He was surprised, but they said, *"Don't be afraid! We have a problem (for you to solve) involving one doing wrong against the other. Judge between us truthfully, and don't treat us unfairly. Guide us to the correct way."* [21-22]

"*This man,*" (the first person said), "*is my brother. He has ninety-nine sheep, while I have only one. Yet, one day he said to me, 'Hand it over to me!' and he was mean when he said it.*" [23]

(David, without even hearing the other man's side of the story, quickly made his decision,) saying, "*He's done you wrong by demanding that your sheep be added to his flock. There are for sure many (business) partners who wrong each other, except for those who believe (in Allah) and do what's right, but there aren't many like that!*"

Then Dawud realized that We were testing him, and he asked forgiveness from his Lord (for giving his decision without hearing the other man's side of the story). He bowed down and repented deeply. [24]

Then We forgave him for that (hastiness), and (soon) he'll have close access to Us in a wonderful place of welcome. [25]

Dawud! We made you a caretaker on the earth, so judge between people in truth. Don't follow (your own) whims, for they'll mislead you from the path of Allah.

Those who stray from the path of Allah will find a sad punishment because they forgot about the Day of Account. [26]

After a long time the old books

Of Allah were lost or changed

Allah sent a new Messenger

Who was 'Esa or Jesus by name

He tried to bring back true religion

But his people didn't listen

They attacked him

And tried hard to stop his mission

'Esa was not able to change his people

Next Allah chose another brave boy

To be His Messenger

This boy was named Muhammad (p)

Peace be upon him

He lived in Arabia

A dry and dusty place

Soon his religion would

Spread all over the place

The followers of Muhammad (p) are found all over the world!

Muhammad (p) also had very hard

Challenges and problems to face

Most of his people believed in idols

And used to do very bad things

After a lot of struggles

Islam became the religion of the land

And because of this effort

We all proudly stand

The people who wanted to keep their idols attacked Muhammad (p) and his followers a lot

We are the followers of Muhammad (p)

We believe in the religion of Islam

This is the way of life Allah gave us

To help us beat the Shaytan!

A follower of Islam is a Muslim!

Allah will send no more books

For He promised to save the Qur'an

Allah bless Prophet Muhammad (p)

Who gave us our Islam!

We study the life of the Prophet Muhammad (p)
So we can learn how to be good Muslims

All the Prophets and Messengers taught the same five basic things:

Allah is One. Help the poor. Be good. Pray and fast. Remember life is short.

What is the Last Day?

The world cannot go on forever

People have lived

And died over and over

Great kingdoms arose and fell

Heroes and bad guys came as well

We learn in school about the people of the past

In our own lives we struggle and strive

We juggle our money,

And dreams and try to survive

But Allah has promised that

There will come a day

When He will order a trumpet to play

That will be the signal to close the show

The world will be over

It will be time to go!

We have a lot to worry about in our own lives

Who will we be? What will we do?

Can we make a good life to live?

One day the sky will open up

The Last Day will be here!

The people did not expect it

But it will come so near!

Allah said the sky will open up as if it had gates!

The universe will start to melt

In every direction it will be felt

This is the Last Day of Life for all!

This is the day where it will all fall!

Allah made the universe with a time limit!
He has a plan for what comes next!

The earth will start to shake

The land will move and quake

The oceans will boil and bake

The Day of Judgment is our fate!

People will cry and run in fear

The earth will break and shatter here

The scared families will run away

Nowhere will be safe on that scary day

The Qur'an says people will be in a panic!
This is called the Last Day

The souls of the dead will be called

Out of their graves they will come

Everyone who ever lived will arise

To the Day of Judgment will they fly!

When people die, their life energy does not go away. Their souls sleep until Allah will call them back.

Now every soul will come to its place -

The plain of judgment

No one can be late!

This is the time when we see our deeds

This is the day when we learn our fate

People will gather in front of the Throne of Allah so their deeds and actions from their lives can be examined. This is where we get our report card grade for living our life!

Surah 81, Ayat 1-29
How will the World End?

In the Name of Allah,
the Caring, and the Merciful

When the sun is covered in darkness,
When the stars are thrown down,
When the mountains pass away, [1-3]

When the livestock heavy with young are left alone,
When the wild beasts are bunched together,
When the seas rise, [4-6]

When the souls are sorted,
When the baby girl buried alive is asked
For what crime she was killed, [7-9]

When the scrolls are opened,
When the sky is laid bare,
And when Hell is set ablaze and Paradise is brought near,
Then every soul will know what it has prepared. [10-14]

And so, by the (stars) that go back, move on or hide, and by the night as it draws to a close and the dawn as it slowly exhales, (by these signs you must know that) this is the speech of an honored message-bringer. [15-19]

He (Angel Jibraeel) has authority and status before the Lord of the throne, and he is to be obeyed and trusted. [20-21]

Your companion (Muhammad) is not crazy, nor has he been tricked, because he truly did see the (angel of revelation) on the clear horizon. [22-23]

He doesn't hesitate in sharing knowledge of the unseen, nor are these the words of a hated devil. [24-25]

So which way will you go? [26]

This is no less than a reminder to all the worlds, for anyone who seeks to walk the straight path – but not as you want, as Allah wants, the Lord of All the Worlds. [27-29]

---

1. What are two scary things that will happen on the last day?

Our good deeds and bad deeds

Will be compared

They'll be placed on a scale

To see which is greater there

Everything we ever said or did

Will be shown

And in the end we will learn

Where we will go

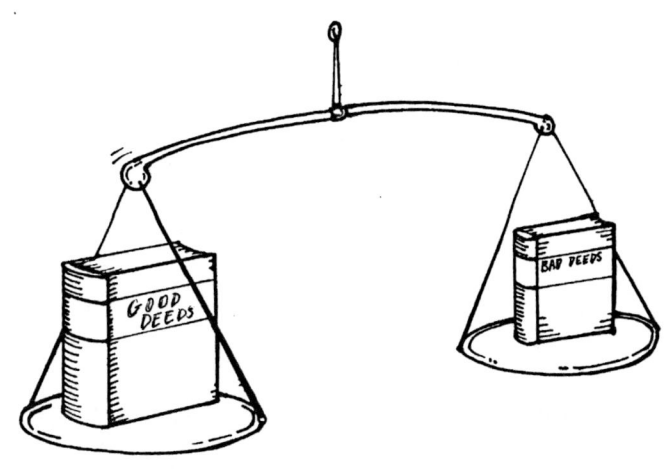

There are a lot of things

Allah may forgive

If we helped others in small ways

We may find many bad deeds erased

But if we were mostly bad

And didn't give a care

When we come back from the judgment

We may be sad and scared

The bad jinns will be judged too

For they whispered bad thoughts

To me and you

Together the bad people

Along with the jinns

Will be pushed in the Fire

To start their punishment within

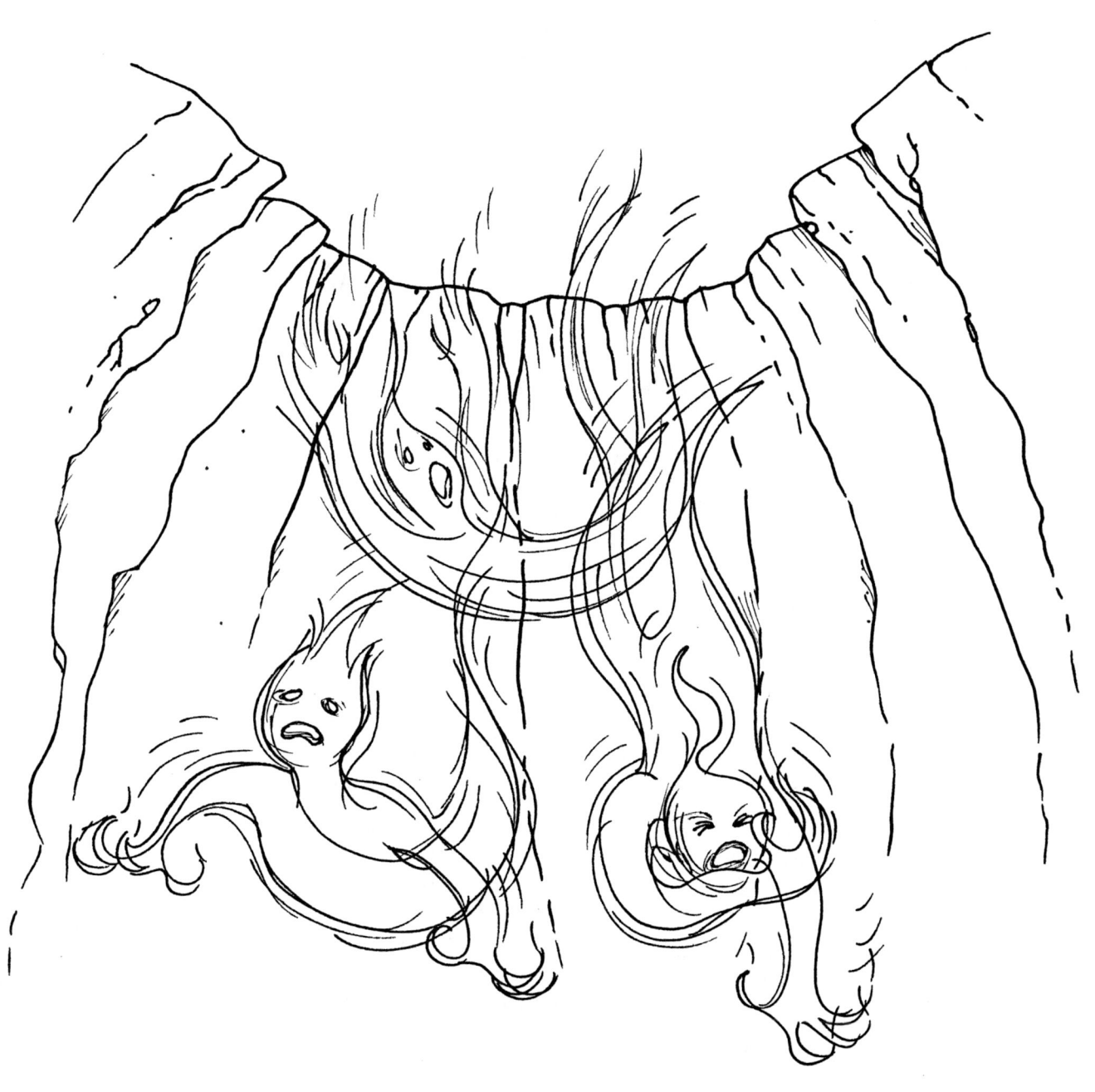

The people who believed in Allah

Will be so happy and so smiley

They were the people

Who did good in their lives

Hoping for Allah's reward

They will all go to Jannah,

To a great and happy Paradise

We should all wish to be them

So we can live forever more!

Prophet Muhammad (p) said that one of the things that gets us into Paradise is if our hearts are attached to the Masjid!

How Does Allah Measure Our Lives?

Allah created people

Our job is to worship Him

We live our lives and do our best

So be sure to Remember Him

Everything is measured

We don't know the future or past

Allah knows what we will get

So be thankful for what you can have

153

There are good days in our lives

Sometimes everything goes our way

Things you never expected

Just seem to come today

When we're safe and happy

And everything seems fine

We mustn't forget Allah

Who gave us our good times

Other days life is too hard

Nothing seems to work

Disasters and endless problems

Always seem to lurk

Why are some days so good

While others seem so bad?

Is there a reason for this?

Were we supposed to be so sad?

Strange things happen every day

Sometimes life is very hard

Allah may be testing us, or trying to make us stronger

The truth is life is measured

We get both the good and bad

Allah wants to test us

To show us that we can

Sometimes He gives us a lot

Will we be thankful or act so bad?

Sometimes He takes precious things away

Will we be patient or sad?

Surah 10, Ayat 4-10
How does a Muslim Think about Life?

In the Name of Allah,
the Caring, and the Merciful

All of you will return back to Him, and Allah's promise is true. He's the One Who started the process of creation and then repeats it, so that He can fairly reward those who believe and do what's right.

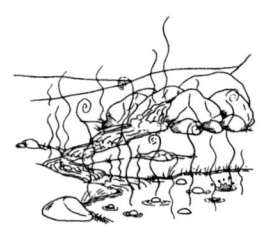

Those who reject Him will be forced to drink boiling muck, and they'll have a painful punishment because of their rejection. [4]

He's the One Who made the sun glow brightly with multiple (colors in splendor) and the moon to be lit up. He measured out (the moon's) stations, so you could keep track of the years and the passage (of time).

Allah didn't create (all of these things) except for a real reason, and He explains His verses to people who understand. [5]

Truly, in the switching of night and day and in everything that

Allah created in the heavens and the earth - there are proofs for those who are mindful (of Him). [6]

Those who don't look forward to their meeting with Us, who are satisfied with the life of this world and who ignore Our (revealed) verses - they're going to have their home in the Fire because of what they've earned for themselves. [7-8]

However, those who believe and do what's right – they will be guided by their Lord because of their faith – rivers will flow beneath them in gardens of delight! [9]

Their prayer within (the garden) will be, "*Glory be to You, O Allah!*"

Their greeting will be, "*Peace,*" and they'll end their prayers by saying, "*Praise be to Allah, the Lord of All the Worlds!*" [10]

---

1. Look at the first paragraph. Allah gives a reason why He made the creation. What is the reason?

2. Where can we find proof of Allah and His power?

3. How will people end their prayers in the garden? What will they say?

Allah gives people choices

Of how they want to act

Will they remember Him at all times

Or be bad in every task?

Allah decided how long

People get to live

We're not meant to live here forever

Allah has so much more to give

People have choices to make.
We have very little control over what
happens around us, but we do control how we
feel and respond to the events of our lives.
Remember Allah in good times and bad!

All people must leave this earth

Our souls will soon be free

Our job here is to be

The best that we can be

That's why Allah brings times

Both of good and bad

So we can learn to truly be

Thankful for what we had

Life is like a circle

We're born and grow and die

Our job is not to build forever

Our home is in the sky

Allah measured all things

Our life, our jobs and more

He doesn't make us act

But gives us choices to explore

All people follow the same circle of life.

This life is like a big school, and Allah sent Books and Messengers to help us pass the test.

On the Day of Judgment we will get our grades!

Allah did not leave us

To struggle on our own

He sent us many guidebooks

And Messengers to show!

Allah gave us the teachings

And the practices to do

To make us better people

A straight path for me and you!

Can you name these practices that make us better people?

Allah is always watching

His angels are always there

He loves us to remember Him

Here and everywhere

He wants us to always be good

Not to lie or cheat or steal

And He wants us to talk about Him

So more people know He's real

Allah gave people the choice to accept Him or not.
When He told Shaytan that people were better,
It was because people had the power
to accept Him from faith alone.
The jinns did not have this power.

Word Search
How to Live a Good Life

```
P X G U L E N V R X R S
R I Y N O M I T S E T H
D E L Z O E D J S A Q A
E N Y G R P Y J I E G H
D P I A R H E A Y K N A
G X O K R I A H A G I D
M G I H X P M L M A T A
H A K A Z Q Q A A W S H
E C N E I T A P G S A Z
C H A R I T Y S U E F W
G O O D H A P P Y D K J
F X Y I V T Q M A L S I
```

Names to Find and Circle

The words can be in any direction!

Hint: look for the first two letters of a word together!

CHARITY, FASTING, GOOD, HAJJ, HAPPY, HOPE, ISLAM, KIND, PATIENCE, PILGRIMAGE, PRAYER, SALAH, SHAHADAH, SIYAM, TESTIMONY, ZAKAH

Be thankful for the boring and normal days
This is when you are safe and happy.
Never forget that Allah is your final protector
Who can give you strength on the hard days.

How Do I Thank Allah?

Think about the things you are thankful for in your life. Make a list of three things that you think are blessings from Allah for you.

1. _____

2. _____

3. _____

Now write a letter to Allah explaining why you are happy with His blessings in your life. Be sure to provide examples of what He gave you, and be sure to say thank you! Write your letter in the space below. Start by writing, "Dear Allah,"

How is Life in the Next World?

All people will be brought

To Judgment Day

They will see all their actions

Like watching a play

The bad people will be sad and cry

Because they said the fire was a lie

But it was true and now there's no escape

There's just one road left for them to take

The good people will be happy that day

They know that Paradise is only a step away

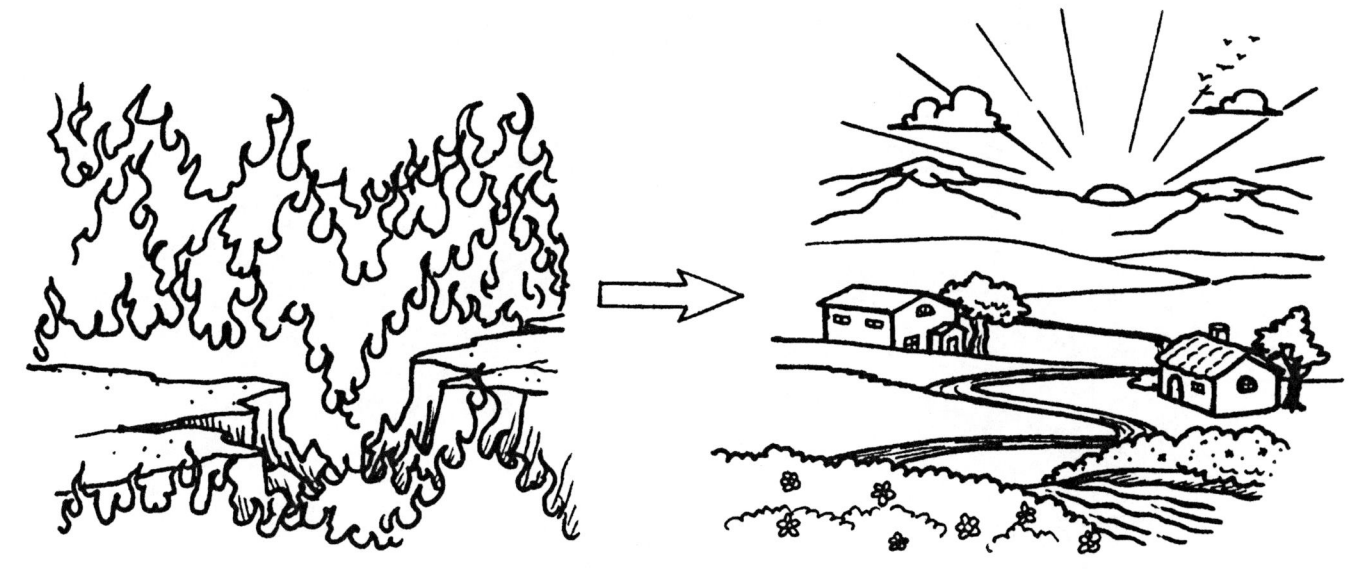

The Day of Judgment will last for 50,000 years!

So many people loved their treasures

They lied and stole and failed to measure

They ignored the warnings

in their heart and soul

They thought of nothing more than gold

Let them try to keep it safe

In the fire they will lose even their own face!

A life spent in love of more

Is built on a lie – a lie for sure!

The Fire – Jahannam it is called,

That is where they'll finally lose it all!

Allah calls the Fire the hottest place

It is punishment for the bad people

The people who loved to waste

It is so hot it feels like ice!

Everyone is alone and that's not nice

Some people who were not all bad

May one day come out and stop being sad

But the worst people of all

The ones who did the biggest crimes

They may stay in their forever for all times

The Fire is 70 times hotter than any fire on earth

Allah created a beautiful Garden

The souls of the good people enter in joy

They believed in Allah

And showed that they cared

And it's filled with light everywhere

No soul will ever feel any pain

Everyone will be young again

The angels will sing and the people will pray

Thanking Allah each and every day

The good people will have all they desire

They were the ones

Who were saved from the Fire

They controlled themselves

On Earth and they prayed

Now it's their turn to feel happy everyday

Everyone will have a mansion

Filled with treasures

Couches and pillows and food on gold platters

Every kind of yummy thing will be there

This is for you, O soul who had cared!

Surah 52, Ayat 21-28
What is It Like in Paradise?

In the Name of Allah,
the Caring, and the Merciful

Those who believe and whose relatives follow them in belief will be reunited (in Paradise) with their family.  We won't deprive them of (the value) of their (good) deeds, although everyone is responsible only for his own actions. [21]

We'll give them fruit and meat and anything else they desire.

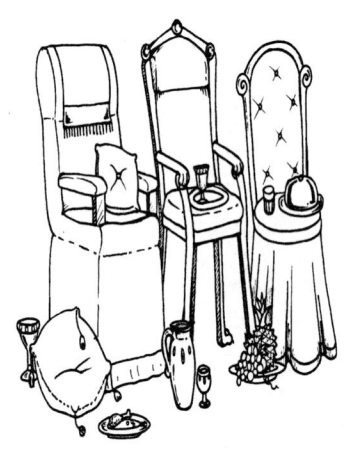 They'll pass around a cup (of sweet drink) that doesn't make people start to talk nonsense or get wild. [22-23]

All around them youths will go
    about (serving them), and
    their (appearance will)
    remind them of expensive pearls. [24]

They'll walk up to each other and ask
    about (new) things. [25]

They'll say, *"We used to worry about our families before, though Allah was good to us and protected all of us from the punishment of the searing heat. We used to call upon Him before (in our lives on earth), and He certainly is Benevolent and Merciful."* [26-28]

---

1. Who do we get to see in Paradise?

2. What is one nice thing we get to do there?

3. What will the people talk about in Paradise?

We won't be alone in our green Paradise

We'll be joined by friends and family

Won't that be so nice!

All those who believed will be right there

That's why it's important that you always share

Tell people how to get to Jannah today

If you love your friends

You won't throw them away

Everyone in Jannah will live forever

This is the promise your Lord will deliver!

Our job in life is to be good and say

Allah is my God and to Him do I pray

The Shaytan will try to use all his tricks

Fight him with everything – even use sticks!

Enjoy your time and love all those you can

Just never forget you live in Allah's plan

If you have faith and avoid bad deeds

Allah has promised forever for you

In a Garden we cannot yet see!

Be a good Muslim
and show Allah you're true!

The Holy Qur'an is Allah's last Book

It is a really good Book – just take a look!

It teaches us how to be honest and good

It is our guidebook for all that we should

Learn about the last Prophet

Whenever you can

His example is inspiring,

He was a beautiful man

Islam is our religion,

It means following Allah's will

So be the best Muslim you can be,

And He'll reward you with His Mercy!

The Qur'an has 114 chapters

Some chapters are long and some are short

Read some every day if you can

You get rewards from Allah if you do!

Other Books for Young Readers
Go to www.ifna.net/bookstore.htm or www.mymuslimbookstore.com for more

Full Circle: Story and Coloring Book
By Yahiya Emerick

What do you do when... Rashid is going to the Masjid for prayer. But on the way he finds an old woman who needs help. If he helps her, he will be late for prayer. If he does not help her, he will miss doing a good deed. Should he help the old woman or should he get to prayer on time? Find out what he does in this wonderful story about going full circle. A strong moral tale showing young children how to continue to do good deeds even when they are worried about keeping other responsibilities. Illustrated. Ages 4-8

Allah Made the World
By Samina Najar

A full color picture book showing the vast world that Allah made with delightful, rhyming couplets and questions for thought. Illustrated. Ages 3-8

Ibrahim's Search
By Qasim Najar

Where is Allah? Ibrahim is a young boy who goes out on a quest to find Allah. What he finds is a delightful lesson in true faith. Illustrated, full color. Ages 4-8

Little Jana's Big Surprise
By Qasim Najar

When a group of orphans are entrusted with running their uncle's farm, the boys take charge leaving little Jana alone and without help. She quickly devises a plan of her own and shows the boys that there is more to little girls than meets the eye! Illustrated, full color. Ages 4-8

The Meaning of the Holy Qur'an for School Children
Produced by Yahiya Emerick

This is a translation – with *asbab ul nuzool* – of the ENTIRE Qur'an for young readers. It has clever and engaging pictures and graphics and is the only book of its kind available today. 828 pages. Ages 8 and up.